Wake Up and SELL

Wake Up and SELL

Written By Theresa Gale and Mary Anne Wampler

Note for Librarians: a cataloguing record for this book that includes
Dewey Decimal Classification and US Library of Congress numbers
is available from the National Library of Canada. The complete
cataloguing record can be obtained from the National Library's online
database at:
www.nlc-bnc.ca/amicus/index-e.html
ISBN 1-4120-3583-X
Printed in Victoria, BC, Canada

TRAFFORD

Offices in Canada, USA, Ireland, UK and Spain
This book was published *on-demand* in cooperation with Trafford
Publishing. On-demand publishing is a unique process and service of
making a book available for retail sale to the public taking advantage
of on-demand manufacturing and Internet marketing. On-demand
publishing includes promotions, retail sales, manufacturing, order
fulfilment, accounting and collecting
royalties on behalf of the author.
Book sales in Europe:
Trafford Publishing (UK) Ltd., Enterprise House, Wistaston Road
Business Centre, Wistaston Road, Crewe CW2 7RP UNITED KINGDOM
phone 01270 251 396 (local rate 0845 230 9601)
facsimile 01270 254 983; info.uk@trafford.com
Book sales for North America and international:
Trafford Publishing, 6E–2333 Government St.,
Victoria, BC V8T 4P4 CANADA
phone 250 383 6864 (toll-free 1 888 232 4444)
fax 250 383 6804; email to bookstore@trafford.com

www.trafford.com/robots/04-1411.html

10 9 8 7 6 5 4

Contents

Acknowledgments vii

A Note from the Authors ix

Introduction xi

Chapter One: Why the Enneagram? 1
Chapter Two: Basic Enneagram Concepts 5
Chapter Three: Discovering Your Style Quiz 13
Chapter Four: Steps to Discovering Your Style...................19
Chapter Five: Description of the Nine Enneagram Styles......23
    Style 1 24
    Style 2 30
    Style 3 36
    Style 4 42
    Style 5 48
    Style 6 53
    Style 7 58
    Style 8 63
    Style 9 69

Chapter Six: Now that I Know My Style, What Do I Do? 75

About Transform, Inc...80

Acknowledgments

We want to acknowledge all those individuals who have helped in the making of *Wake-Up and Sell!*

Helen Palmer who has been our teacher and friend on our journey. We appreciate the hard work she has done to make the Enneagram teachings available to the public. She has always been supportive of our work and has encouraged us to bring these teachings to the workplace. For that and her continued love, we are grateful.

David Daniels was the first of our teachers to bring the Enneagram to the Stanford School of Business. The course, Leadership and the Enneagram, offered to MBA students, modeled how the Enneagram can be applied in the workplace and the extraordinary results that can be achieved when leaders commit to self-discovery as a way of life. For David's teachings and his continued support, we are grateful.

To our many clients who have embraced the Enneagram and allowed us to introduce it to their organizations. We have learned together and for that we are grateful.

To Bernardine Abbott, Theresa's mother, who spent hours editing this book. For her belief in our work and her sharing her gift with us, we are grateful.

A Note from the Authors

Many have wondered why our first book about the Enneagram deals with the topic of sales. The Enneagram, as you will see, is first and foremost a tool for self-discovery and personal growth and development. Whether in leadership, working on a team, managing a project, working with clients or selling to prospects, understanding yourself is the first step to effectiveness in any of these areas.

In working with organizations, we have found that teaching sales people the Enneagram gets the fastest return on investment than any other organizational effort. Without a doubt, more sales allow organizations to grow and thrive. When salespeople improve their results, the whole company benefits!

As much as I, Mary Anne, love consulting, training and coaching, to this very day it still thrills me to be sitting with a prospect or client, listening to their problems, exploring desires for their business, asking just the right question to discover what's really going on, designing a solution and closing the deal. It's fun, it's thrilling, it's real and it matters.

I clearly remember my Dad asking me after my first few years as a sales trainer, "When are you going to get a real job?" It was in my automatic response to him when I truly understood the importance that selling and being a sales trainer holds. My response was simply, "Nothing happens in business until some-one sells something."

Transform's success, in large part, comes from an understanding of the crucial role that sales plays in a business's success. Both of us began working with the Enneagram for personal reasons. As we learned about ourselves and saw the huge shifts that were happening for us in our personal lives, we began to introduce it into the work we were doing with salespeople, managers, teams and individuals. What we found was that by introducing the Enneagram at the beginning of a training or coaching effort, the learning/change curve was shortened, results came quicker and newly acquired skills and behaviors were embraced and implemented more consistently over longer periods of time.

Selling is an art that takes skill, integrity and wisdom. It is a profession where effective, open communication is paramount, where relationships are forged, problems are solved and possibilities become reality. What we have learned in working with the Enneagram in sales is that:

- It's about choice.
- It's about showing up.
- It's about interactions.
- It's about building relationships.
- And it all begins and ends with self-understanding.

Organizations that invest in the personal growth and development of their salespeople reap the most rewards!

Theresa and Mary Anne

Introduction

There are thousands of books on the market that teach people how to sell, but few address the inner state of a salesperson as they attempt to execute the tactics and strategies taught by the experts. We wonder what goes on inside the salesperson as they attempt to make a cold call for the first time; or, pull up to the guarded entrance of a *Fortune* 100 company and press to meet with the facilities manager even though they don't have an appointment; or, stop a colleague in the midst of a presentation to a board of directors because the colleague has gone way off the agenda; or, finally, ask for a decision when the decision maker wants to "think it over."

Salespeople must be at the top of their game when in front of a prospect or client and yet, all too often, they are on automatic and operating out of habitual patterns that are often unconscious. These habitual patterns of behavior may or may not support success in the moment of engagement with a client or prospect. Let's look at an example of how this works. A salesperson named Peter is getting ready for an appointment with a qualified prospect whom he doesn't know. Just before the appointment, Peter's sales manager tells him that Peter needs to find out the client's budget for the project they are going to be discussing. Peter has run into problems before by avoiding conversations about budget.

Internally, everything inside Peter says "There is no way I can do this—it feels impolite to talk about money at the first appointment. I don't even have a relationship with him yet. I know I should do it but I've tried to do it before and I can't get myself to talk about money. I don't understand why we can't just write the proposal. By that time I'll have a stronger, better relationship and we can work out pricing issues then." Peter believes this to be true even though he has lost several big deals because his prospects were shocked when they saw the final numbers.

What's going on here? Peter likes to focus on building a strong relationship, sometimes too strong, before talking about money. He believes that people have to like him to buy from him so asking about money too soon will turn people off. So here he is, the internal chatter is resisting but the external reality is that he can not walk out of the appointment without the information his sales manager wants. How do you think he "shows up" in that sales call? Where is his attention? What non-verbal signals is he sending during the sales call? If building a relationship is where his attention habitually goes during sales calls, how can he do this successfully when he knows he must step out of his comfort zone and at some point, from his perspective, break rapport to ask about the budget?

Some seasoned salesperson might say, "Just get over it and ask about the budget" or, "What a wimp, he's not gonna cut it in sales." But what we know is that Peter has a great track record and is a very successful sales rep. He hits quotas, his customers keep coming back and they refer others to him and he rarely has complaints. Why? Because he is so astute at building strong relationships that his clients do like him and trust him implicitly. So what's the problem? Besides his sales manager's concerns that Peter may lose the deal, the challenge Peter faces personally is that he is working 12-hour days and it takes him at least three appointments to close a sale when other reps are closing in one or two. His sales manager believes that if Peter can just speed up the sales process by asking some key questions in the first appointment, he'll get to the close sooner and not burn out because of the hours he is working.

Our experience in working with sales professionals over 15 years tells us that changing behavior is not about just doing different behavior. If that were so, we wouldn't have people living with addictions, bad habits or destructive behaviors. Changing behavior starts with a personal journey inward to uncover one's core motivation and the internal thoughts, habits and emotions that support and hinder selling success. Once an individual understands these patterns and why he does what he does, they have a chance at making a choice as to whether to continue the old patterns and behaviors or to choose a new way—one that supports success. While we all have many behaviors and beliefs that support us, uncovering those that don't in the moment and then choosing a more supportive approach is what we refer to as "waking up."

How can we wake up and choose behaviors that support our selling success? The Enneagram, a powerful system, provides insight into core motivation and offers a prescriptive path for individuals who want to change non-supportive behaviors.

We have used many assessments, profiles and developmental tools over the years, and have found that the Enneagram system is unparalleled in its ability to get at the core issues that hinder personal and professional success. Used in sales, it offers even the most successful sales professional strategies that increase productivity, improve results and build strong and lasting relationships with clients.

We invite you to read this book and learn more about how the Enneagram can support your selling success. In chapter 1, we answer the question, "Why the Enneagram?" and chapter 2 provides an overview of the Enneagram system and its concepts.

In chapter 3, we've provided a short quiz that helps you begin identifying your Enneagram style and in chapter 4 we offer additional tips for discovering your style. Chapter 5 describes each Enneagram style, how the style supports or hinders sales success, and specific strategies for waking up and unleashing greater selling success. We've included a "Wake-Up Challenge" at the end of each style for those who seek to raise their self-observation to the next level and bring about real change in their lives. Chapter 6 offers next steps for ongoing growth and development now that you know your style and what gets in the way of achieving the results you want.

We know from years of our own personal journey and our consulting experience that the journey inward is the only path that guarantees personal and professional success. We encourage you to embrace this inner journey for we guarantee that you will reap a multitude of rewards along the way!

Chapter One

Why the Enneagram?

The Enneagram is a dynamic yet uncannily accurate system that describes nine personality styles. Each style has a distinctive way of thinking, feeling and acting; consequently, each style has its own natural gifts, limitations and "blind spots." Based on the latter premises, it follows that approaches to communication, decision making, teamwork, sales and leadership will differ according to personality style.

Why the Enneagram?

One of the values of the Enneagram lies in its ability to give insight into the some of the whys of human behavior. For instance, while some salespeople may have difficulty in asking for the sale (a behavior), the reasons why (motivations) are probably different. Many personality systems on the market today, for example, Myers-Briggs, DISC, The Big Five, are insightful and useful for differing reasons. However, in our opinion, the Enneagram is unique in helping the seeker gain insight into personal motivation and in deepening understanding of action or avoidance. In the process of understanding core motivations, each individual begins to know the self on a progressively higher level.

Another value of the Enneagram is that it radically shatters individual perceptions and judgments of other people's intentions and reasons for behaviors. The Enneagram teaches nine different lenses or ways of interpreting the world. With a particular lens or style, an individual interprets situations, events, encounters and experiences from a lens that usually is unexamined rather than one of conscious choice. According to this personality system, there are eight other ways of viewing the same situation, yet people often believe that their interpretation is the right or only way. Learning the Enneagram has the potential to expand the individual's understanding of an interaction or dialogue in the here and now so that distinctly different points of view can be recognized, understood and respected.

Furthermore, one realizes that their interpretation of a given situation may not truly reflect the intentions of another, and, therefore, assumptions and actions may be based on incomplete or incorrect information. Insights gained from the Enneagram help people avoid miscommunications, misunderstandings and inaccurate assumptions. Stated positively, the Enneagram provides the insights and skills for more effective communication and human interaction.

A third value of the Enneagram lies in its ability to reveal individual barriers to success while at the same time offering a pathway for continual learning, development and professional and personal growth. Additionally, a heightened awareness of what is needed to reach one's highest potential and the attainment of life's goals are among the many gains the Enneagram experience offers.

How does knowing your Enneagram Style help you?

The habitual responses an individual has learned and automatically performs may not always result in the desirable or necessary results or outcomes. A person might be wondering, "Why do I always get myself into situations in which I promise the customer something I'm not always certain we can deliver just because the customer wants it?" or, "Why is it so hard to say 'no'?" Another may say, "Why is it that, even though I have the best intentions to be on time, I always seem to over-schedule myself and I am constantly running late for appointments?" While both of these scenarios may originate in people with good intentions, the results may have unintended negative impact on others and, most significantly, on the self.

Again, one might wonder why they had a particular reaction to a person or in a specific situation and, in retrospect, regret outcomes and behaviors. The latter seems to be a fairly common human experience. Therefore, we believe that knowing one's Enneagram style is helpful not only in the understanding of style and habitual patterns of thinking, acting and feeling, but also in recognizing the "triggers" that set the patterns into action. Armed with Enneagram information, one can develop useful strategies for the prevention of unwanted reactions and responses. This level of awareness, learned through the ability to self-observe, helps one to choose action in any given situation or moment. Becoming free of the need for apologies or feelings of guilt after the fact is one of the goals and benefits of learning one's style.

How does all this apply to sales?

The salesperson is constantly engaged in building relationships, influencing people, communicating and interacting with others. To fully comprehend that a prospect or client may, in fact, experience the same situation differently is of critical importance. When an individual becomes highly attuned to this reality, their approach shifts to a more intentional, conscious sales process, one that focuses on real understanding and creating clear, easy communication, relationships and win-win results. Gaining an understanding of the different views/lens of interactions with prospects or clients, and triggers for unwanted reactions, enhances the salesperson's ability to feel good about the self, to stay in control of the selling process and to increase significantly the chances of interacting successfully in business and personal relationships.

In summation, gaining a solid understanding of one's personal style, strengths, limitations and blind spots, and one's impact on others, and vice versa—all of these considerations provide the first steps along the pathway to greater selling and personal success.

Chapter Two

Basic Enneagram Concepts

To fully understand and appreciate the value of the Enneagram teachings in personal and professional development, it is important to review the basic concepts of the Enneagram system and model.

1. The term Enneagram comes from Greek origins with "Ennea" meaning nine and "gram" meaning model. The Enneagram is, therefore, a nine-pointed model.

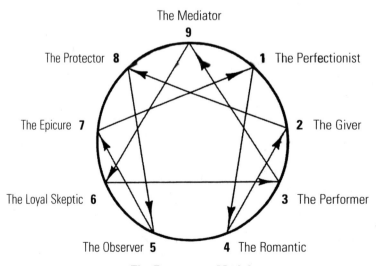

The Enneagram Model

2. No one style is better than another.

3. The Enneagram describes nine ways of thinking about, viewing and interacting in the world. The "lens" we use filters information in a particular way and may limit how we perceive and define situations. The Enneagram shows us that our personality is on automatic and has a habit of mind that operates all the time. In effect, we live in a "personality box."

   The Enneagram helps us get out of that box by teaching us to recognize the habit of mind, especially if it is not working for us. In addition, it gives us the insights necessary to transform this habit into conscious thoughts, feelings and actions that support desired and deserved successes.

4. Our style was developed early in childhood as a way to cope with our environment. The question of how we developed our style always arises when introducing this tool. While there is no definitive answer, the general belief is that all of us come into this world with some predisposition (*heredity/nature*) to our style. However, each individual's environment (*nurture*) reinforces his or her predisposition to operate from one of the lenses described by the Enneagram model.

5. While we have characteristics of all the styles, there is one that is "home base," one that will resonate more strongly with you than the others. Furthermore, this style does not change in essence throughout our lifetime. However, we naturally develop strategies for overcoming the barriers of our style as we mature and age through life experiences. We may also learn to take on characteristics of other styles under certain situations.

6. Looking at the model you will notice that there is an inner triangle made up of points **3, 6** and **9**. These points or styles represent the core points of the Enneagram model with all other styles being a variation of these three points.

7. When looking at the model, one can begin to distinguish between the styles when closely observing the manner in which the different styles filter and process information. In recent years, Western psychology suggests that we have three centers of intelligence through which we process information—the intelligence of the heart (emotional intelligence), of the mind (mental intelligence), and of the body (sensations and instincts).

   Looking at the Enneagram model, the core points, **3, 6** and **9** each anchor a center of intelligence. The **2, 3** and **4** styles are the heart triad. The **5, 6** and **7** styles are the mental or thinking triad, and the **8, 9** and **1** make up the body triad.

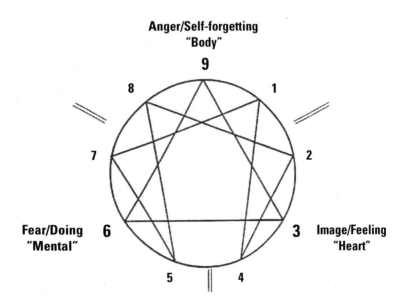

8. The **2**, **3** and **4** styles are called the Heart or Image types. The commonality these three styles share is the way they process and filter information through the heart or emotional center. When information is presented, it is filtered and processed through the emotions. The 2, 3 and 4 styles are concerned with relationships, how one perceives others and how others perceive them. While all of us have access to emotional intelligence, these three styles are attuned more closely to the emotions and engage the emotions to process information.

   The **5**, **6** and **7** styles are called the Head, Thinking or Fear styles. These styles filter information through the mental processes. Information comes in and is analyzed by thinking, sorting, organizing and processing. The 5, 6 and 7 styles are concerned with order, logic, certainty and structure. They are also called the Fear types because each style seeks avoidance of fear through the mental processes of analyzing, planning, organizing and sorting of data.

   The **8**, **9** and **1** styles are called the Body or Anger types. These styles tend to filter information through the intelligence of kinesthetic and physical sensations and gut instinct. Styles 8, 9 and 1 occur as a sense of knowing based upon the physical or gut reactions experienced. These types are also called the Anger types because each of the three styles uses the *energy* of anger to achieve what it is they want or need.

9. The arrows on the model indicate movement of each style when under stress or security. The style moves *with* the arrow in times of stress and *against* the arrow in times of security (when things are going right and you are feeling really good about yourself). The movement to the stress or

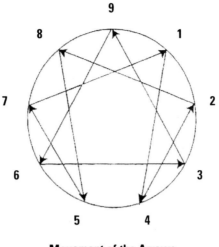

Movement of the Arrows
With Arrow—Stress
Away from Arrow—Security

security point does not mean you become that style, but rather, you take on the characteristics of that style. If you are a 9, the Mediator, in times of stress, you move with the arrow toward the 6 position. You don't become a 6, but from the 9 position you may become doubtful of your abilities, look to worst-case scenarios and become obsessive in thinking over your options or next steps. All of the latter takes place in the head.

In times of security, the 9 moves to the 3 position, taking on the characteristics of the 3, that is, an ability to focus on results, to have clarity about what you are trying to achieve and to attain thorough engagement in the process.

10. Self-observation is the key to identifying style. The best practice is to begin observing yourself as you go through the day, as you interact with others, as you react and respond to

situations that arise and also as you are relaxing. In becoming self-reflective, you can raise your level of awareness and begin to understand how your style helps or hinders your personal and professional successes.

11. No one but *you* can identify your style. Other people may be able to provide input or feedback as to how you impact those with whom you interact, but ultimately you are the expert on your style. You are the only one who knows what drives you, where your attention goes, what thoughts, assumptions, attitudes, etc., drive your behavior.

12. It is accepted good practice not to type others whether intentionally or in jest or fun. Nor do you use your style or other styles as a way to explain or justify questionable behaviors and motivations. It can be damaging, hurtful and limiting to view others in their personality box. In speaking of others in terms of 9s, 6s and 3s and all other numbers of the Enneagram, one must remember that this is done for the sake of convenient language in an attempt to understand this personality system. One must always bear in mind the fact that a mere number can never fully describe a person, a being who is always much more that the description of a number.

The essential value of the Enneagram, then, lies in the realization that the only way each person comes to understand another person is through interaction and dialogue. We need to ask questions about how the other person is seeing a particular situation. Only then can we present our own lens, not as truth, but as one way to view a situation. When all members in an organization receptively adhere to this practice, relationships will be enhanced, personal responsibility increased and underlying issues discussed in a non-threatening, non-defensive manner.

By being aware of ourselves (our thoughts, reactions, feelings and so forth) in the moment, we can choose a different way of being in the moment with others.

Rather than reactive and on automatic, we are present and choosing how we want to impact others.
In essence, we are awake!

Chapter Three

Discovering Your Style Quiz

The "Nine Approaches to Sales" Quiz

There is no definitive test that reveals what style you are; rather, discovering your style can only be done by you. However, the quiz below can be a starting point for your discovery. Read the nine paragraphs below. As you are reading the paragraphs identify the one or ones that best describe you. There may be a few that are close so just put a star next to all that you think best describe you. Then follow the directions provided on page 18.

1. I have very high standards for how I should interact with my prospects or clients. I am ethical in how I represent my company and the products and services it offers, and I believe a prospect needs to make the right buying decision whether that is to buy from me or from another company. I may get too technical in a sales call but I just believe that the prospect or client needs to be informed before they buy something. I like structure, chains of command, policies and procedures to be spelled out and become irritated, even

angry, when others don't follow procedures and processes. I work very hard, sometimes to the point of exhaustion, to get things right or correct. I tend to notice what's wrong a lot and feel it's my duty to point out error whenever I see it. I am results-oriented and expect a lot from myself. I pay attention to details and tend to focus on the details with a prospect or client. I sometimes have trouble building rapport with prospects and clients. It's not right to ask personal questions during a sales call. Others have told me I am too critical or picky but I'm just trying to make things right.

2. Relationships are what sales and selling is all about. I have an uncanny ability to know what prospects and clients need even before they even realize it. It's important for prospects and clients to like me and I believe that if they like me, they will do business with me. What really motivates me is helping people and building relationships—making money is the reward for doing that. I take pride in the fact that my clients couldn't do it without me and they tell me that all the time. I like to associate with people who are influential and can help me achieve my goals. I probably spend too much time with bonding and rapport and often leave a sales call not having gotten the information I needed or asking for the prospect's business. It's difficult for me to ask for money or say no to a prospect or client, especially when they want something that I or the company can't really provide. I get angry or resentful when I help someone and they don't help me out when I need it.

3. Sales is about results—I am only as good as the results I produce. I am results-oriented. I love to compete, to win and to be recognized for what I achieve. Winning a sale is an

adrenaline rush especially when I've won over my competition. I want results and sometimes skip over the details or cut corners to get to the end result. When I walk into a sales call, I know the results I want and I go for it even if it means having to gloss over the details that my company expects me to cover. Sometimes I make promises I can't always keep and that gets me in trouble with prospects, clients and my company. I project a high-profile image and believe it's important to have credentials, be in the right social circles and be concerned with who's who in a crowd. I can easily shift my image to fit any situation. I run all the time, my calendar is always booked and I really don't know how to relax.

4. For me to be successful in sales I need to sell products or services that make a difference, are unique and involve using my creativity. I get bored easily when having to do mundane, repetitive, boring tasks so I just don't do them very often. I get to know my prospects and clients really well and like to connect with them on a deep level. It's important for me to really know them well. I hate small talk or schmoozing and try to avoid it at all costs. People say I am too emotional and let my emotions get in the way of selling. I do have intense feelings and may take things too personally. I sometimes wish I had what other people have and often feel as if I am misunderstood. I am at my best when I am doing creative, unique and meaningful work and feeling as if I am really connected with prospects, my clients and the people with whom I work.

5. I want to have all the information I need to be successful on a sales call. I'm not always comfortable with meeting new people but if I feel prepared I know I can do a good job.

Small talk and bonding are not my strength. I get uncomfortable during a sales call when a prospect gets emotional. I believe that if a prospect is fully informed about the product or service I am selling and sees the logic behind buying it, they will make the best buying decision. I prefer just presenting the facts rather than having to sell someone. Better yet, if I can just submit a proposal and let them make a decision on their own with minimal interaction, that's the best scenario for me.

6. When selling, I prefer to deal with people I know or are referred to. I don't really like cold calling or prospecting. I am skilled at building solid relationships with prospects and clients. Prospects and clients trust me because I'm not afraid to tell them the truth and I won't promise something I can't deliver. I'll also tell the prospect if my product or service isn't right for them. I'm a great troubleshooter and so prospects like me because I can show them the worst case that could happen if they don't find the right solution for them. I have to work on helping them see the positive that can result from buying from me. Prospects buy from me and they know that I will be there with them 150 percent. I sometimes doubt my abilities and this can get in the way of me being successful in sales. I'm more comfortable when I'm solving problems than when I am experiencing success. People say I ask a lot of questions, and I do, but what I'm trying to do is understand the entire situation and see any possible holes in the prospect's or client's thinking that they might not see.

7. I like to work with the movers and shakers in a business or those in high positions of authority. I am very creative in proposing solutions and have the ability to influence

prospects by showing them the possibilities that a solution will bring them. I like big challenges and being involved in initial projects where I am part of developing strategy and plans for how to achieve specific goals. I don't like to talk about problems because every problem has a solution. I like to sell something and then move on to another sales opportunity. It's better to have someone else service an account—I get bored once the sale or challenge of the sale is over. I'm told that I have trouble staying with a project to completion and making commitments. There are so many options out there. The world is rich with possibilities and opportunities so why should I limit myself?

8. I am results-oriented, confident and in charge during the sales call. I am skilled at assessing who the decision makers are and am comfortable selling to those with power. When I go into a sales call I pretty much already know what a prospect needs. I can be forceful when telling a prospect or client what they need. I like honest, straightforward prospects who don't waste my time or beat around the bush. My time is valuable and if they don't like what I have to sell, I'm out of there. People tell me I intimidate them. I'm just doing what I need to do to get results. I get really irritated with prospects who can't make a decision. I might get so impatient, I cross them off the list as a prospect. I know what I want and I go after it.

9. I prefer working with people I know. I am great at creating rapport and making people feel comfortable. I'm a great listener and I can usually really understand what a prospect feels, thinks and wants. I'm pretty intuitive when selling but I really struggle with asking tough questions that I think are too personal or invade another person's privacy. I don't want

them to be upset with me or create any conflict. There are times when I know I need to ask a question but I am so uncomfortable, I just don't do it. If I think a prospect or client is upset with me, I may avoid their calls or work on something else. If I can avoid the conflict I will. I'm really uncomfortable making calls to prospects I don't know unless I've been referred to them.

Directions:

Enter below the number of the paragraph that most describes you as your first choice. Then enter the paragraph number that best describes you as your second choice and, finally, your third choice. You do not have to have three choices. Some individuals recognize themselves immediately as one style and others begin with a few to explore.

First Choice: _____
Second Choice: _____
Third Choice: _____

Continue to chapter 4 and read about steps for discovering your style.

Chapter Four

Steps to Discovering Your Style

Individuals discover their style in a variety of ways. In our experience, some individuals know immediately what their style is while, for perfectly valid reasons, others must engage in a longer process to discover their "home base." There is no one right or correct way to find style—but we can offer some advice.

1. Now that you've gotten a feel for the nine styles and you've identified those paragraphs that best describe you, you are ready to read more about those styles you've identified. Read the brief description of each style you've selected provided on pages 23-73 of this book.

2. While this book focuses on yourself as a salesperson, the Enneagram describes nine distinctive personality styles, so if you struggle with identifying which paragraph best describes you, another approach would be to reflect back on your life, specifically during your teenage years. How would you describe yourself then? What was important to you? What issues did you deal with? How did others perceive you? How

did you perceive others? These questions may be helpful. Our experience has demonstrated that style is mostly on automatic and more obvious during teenage years. Therefore, thinking about those years may be helpful.

3. Another avenue to assist one is thinking about the centers of intelligence—heart, head and body—and asking the following questions: Which center do you utilize most frequently? Which center is least developed? Using this format will at least get you into a center that best fits you. At this point, you will be able to narrow down your choice among the three styles in that particular center. For example, an individual might say, "I am always in my head. I do know that." In this case, the Head center—points 5, 6 or 7—would be the ones to first examine. Another way is to begin by excluding the one or two centers that don't fit. Then hone in on the last one, exploring it further.

4. Think about what happens when you are stressed or when you are feeling secure. When stressed, what thoughts, feelings and actions are prominent? When you are feeling secure, what does that look like in the Enneagram terms? Identifying your stress and security points also helps you to narrow your choices as you work to discover style.

5. As you are trying to discover style, it is critical that you start to raise your level of awareness and observe yourself in situations. Where is your attention? What thoughts are you having? What actions are you taking? Why? What feelings do you have? If no feelings are present, ask yourself why not? How are you impacting others? How do you imagine you are perceived by others? What are you avoiding or not avoiding?

Note again that *self-observation* is the key to discovery of style. You can read a multitude of books, but, typically, it is through self-observation that individuals discover their style.

6. Asking those closest to you how they perceive you is helpful but, as we stated earlier, their perceptions are from their lens, so accept their feedback for the limited perspective that it is. Continue to observe yourself until you discover your style.

7. Lastly, feel free to call in a certified Enneagram teacher who has been trained in how to lead you through a self-discovery process to find your style.

Chapter Five

Description of the Nine Enneagram Styles

There are many written works on the Enneagram System. Three you may want to use to further explore the Enneagram and the nine styles are: *The Essential Enneagram,* by David Daniels and Virginia Price, *The 9 Ways of Working,* by Michael Goldberg and *The Enneagram: Understanding Yourself and Others,* by Helen Palmer. *The Essential Enneagram* helps you identify your style and then provides a brief description of each style. Also included in this resource are useful practices for each style to increase their self-observation skills. *The 9 Ways of Working* provides a straightforward description of the Enneagram and the nine styles as they occur in the working environment. Reading multiple sources on styles helps those who are uncertain of style to gain greater clarity. *The Enneagram: Understanding Yourself and Others* is the most comprehensive and well-known textbook on the Enneagram. It provides the history of the Enneagram, its psychological and spiritual roots and extensive descriptions of each style.

Below is a brief description of each style. For each one, a general overview is provided followed by the strengths and challenges of the style as they relate to selling. Lastly, specific strategies for greater sales success are discussed for each style along with a challenge for those ready to WAKE UP and SELL their way to greater personal and professional success.

Style 1
The Perfectionist

General Characteristics

The Perfectionists are concerned with doing the right things and doing things right. Their attention is drawn to errors and what is or isn't correct. This style typically holds themselves and others to very high standards of excellence yet may not always communicate the standards by which they or others are judged. The Perfectionist style operates effectively when structure, chain of command, policies and procedures and high standards of excellence are clearly defined, refined and enforced. The Perfectionists become irritated and angry when others don't adhere to set standards and typically come across as overly critical and judgmental of others when standards are not met. The Perfectionists have a very active, never-ending inner critic that is constantly judging, comparing and assessing performance. As children, people who claim this style learned that one is loved for being right or perfect—nothing less is acceptable.

Driven by this belief, the 1 style is highly attentive to details, thrives in a structured work environment and is valued on a team for the ability to get things right. The underside of this style is, that in trying to be perfect, the 1 may procrastinate or take longer to do tasks, attempting to make each and every task perfect; may come across as critical and judgmental of others (though not half as critical as they are of themselves) and may be inflexible or rigid in how they view situations. From the 1 perspective, a situation is either right or wrong, black or white; there is little grey area when it comes to right and wrong.

Sales Environment

The 1 personality in sales has an acute attention to details, high standards for how to interact with prospects and clients, is ethical in how they represent the company and the products and services it offers and is highly organized.

Some challenges for this style in selling include:

- Being really hard on themselves and not seeing the value they do bring to a particular situation.
- Having difficulty in building rapport due to focusing on details and tasks rather than the relationship and the emotional needs or wants of the buyer.
- Desiring to give away information or tell the prospect or client how to fix the problem in order to build trust and credibility.
- Becoming too muddled in the details and techno-lingo when describing a problem.
- Telling the prospect or client what they need versus asking probing questions and listening to what the prospect or client wants or needs.
- Trying to force the right way to do something versus offering a service that meets the needs and desires of the prospect or client.
- Not gaining agreement of the term excellence so that both the salesperson and prospect or client know how to measure success.
- Getting irritated or annoyed at the prospect, client or even their own company when things aren't right.
- Having an ethical problem or seeing it as wrong to discuss money and budget with the prospect or client.

- Having a level of discomfort with asking "personal" questions and preferring to talk details and specifics out of their own comfort level.
- Not being responsive to the prospect or client due to making assumptions about what is the "right" way to handle a situation, problem or issue.
- Coming across as stiff, rigid or personally unconcerned.

WAKE-UP Strategies for the 1 Style

1. Be aware of the beliefs you hold regarding being a salesperson, discussing money, asking personal questions and so forth. Make certain that your beliefs support selling success and also align with your organization's values, commitments and beliefs around selling and customer service.

Practice and Application

1. Write down the beliefs that support your work and success as a salesperson.

2. What values, beliefs and commitments do you have in common with your organization? *For example, integrity.*

---

2. Make sure you have a clearly defined sales process that you follow consistently, even if your organization doesn't have one. Following a process helps you stay on track and focused on the outcome.

   A sales process describes the steps taken to sell a prospect from the moment the prospect contacts your company, or you contact them, until services are no longer provided for that client.

Practice and Application

1. Does your organization have a clearly defined sales process? If so, list the steps of that process.

2. If your organization does not have a defined sales process, what process do you go through in selling to a prospect? Define the steps below:
   a.
   b.
   c.
   d.
   e.
   f.
   g.

---

3. Learn to notice when you are locked into a position. For example, often you can notice a pattern when you find yourself thinking, "I know I am right." When this thought is present, ask yourself, "Is there another way to look at this situation? What is the best (not right) way to solve this?"

4. Learn what good enough means. Not everything needs to be done to your standards of perfection. Sometimes getting it done is better then getting it done perfectly. Know the difference between the two.

5. Communicate your expectations to teammates or those who support you so that they clearly know your expectations, and, if you manage them, how you are measuring their performance.

6. Get agreement from prospects and clients on their standards and expectations upfront so that you are on the same page when it comes to measuring success.

7. Just do it! Notice when you are procrastinating or putting off doing a task. Ask yourself, "What's getting in my way of finishing this task?" If you are concerned that the end result won't be perfect, ask yourself, "What would 'good enough' be and can I live with that?"

8. Most importantly, learn to have fun and enjoy selling and approach it like a skillful player playing a fascinating game.

WAKE-UP 30-DAY CHALLENGE

If you really want to see different results, commit to this 30-day challenge and get ready to see transformation before your eyes!

Directions: For the next 30 days, take 15 minutes a day to write down your responses to the questions below. Find a quiet place to write and get yourself a journal to record your thoughts.

Below are two sets of questions. Each day, alternate between the two sets. For example, on day one, respond to Questions 1; on day two respond to Questions 2; on day three respond to Questions 1; on day four respond to Questions 2; and so forth.

Questions 1

1. Where did you notice "error" today? or What went wrong today?

2. Where did you find yourself needing to prove you were right?

3. What could happen if you just let go of being right?

Questions 2

1. What did you do well today?

2. Where and when did your **inner critic** result in self-judgment about what you did or didn't do?

3. In what ways did your self-judgment impact your results today? How did it impact you personally?

Style 2
The Helper

General Characteristics

The Helper is in the Heart Triad and likes to be viewed as helpful to others. This style is primarily focused on key relationships and is often in the position of the power behind the throne. This focus of attention leads to a sense of indispensability and pride in the fact that the Helper is the only one who can meet another person's needs. This style is, in fact, highly intuitive of what others want and need. The 2 style has a belief that success comes from aligning with those who have the power to help the 2 get what they want. There is a quid pro quo established by this dynamic: If I help you, then you will help me. When the latter doesn't happen, primarily because the Helper believes that they shouldn't have to ask for help, this style becomes resentful and angry. The Helper style is highly responsive to approval and encouragement and is typically crushed by disapproval. They like being on a team and can be extremely supportive of leadership and the team if they believe in and support its direction.

The 2 style is motivated by keeping people happy and meeting other's needs. They are highly attentive to relationships and place great emphasis on people, relationships among people, connection to clients, employees and customer service.

Sales Environment

The 2 style in sales has an acute attention to relationships and connection to those who can help them achieve their results. They are usually friendly and outgoing and most people like them. They are highly intuitive about other's needs and see their job as finding ways to meet those needs. While budgets and goals are important, the 2 style is primarily motivated by building successful relationships. Winning the sale is secondary to a well-formed relationship.

The challenges that this style faces in selling include:

- Spends too much time in rapport-building believing that the prospect or client has to like them in order to buy from them.
- Has difficulty asking questions that they feel might upset the prospect or client. Typically these revolve around money, expectations and so forth.
- Overpromises or goes outside the boundaries of service capability in order to be perceived as meeting the needs of the prospect or client. The thinking that prevails is, "I'll figure it out later."
- Misses details such as discussion of costs, timeline for delivery of services, the need for a down payment or discussion of payment terms. The Helper may be so involved in establishing a relationship that they simply run out of time when it comes to details.
- Talks too much, not asking enough questions to get to the real reasons why the prospect or client wants their services or makes assumptions that they know what the prospect or client wants.
- Promises to do something but doesn't write it down and then forgets about it or is too overwhelmed with so many tasks to meet the commitment they made.
- Struggles with closure and moving on from a prospect who doesn't buy; has a hard time closing the file thinking, "we're friends so they might buy from me later."
- Takes a "no" from a prospect or client as a personal affront. This may create resentment and anger that they've given so much and the prospect or client didn't come through with what they needed.

WAKE-UP Strategies for the 2 Style

1. Be aware of the beliefs you hold regarding being a salesperson, discussing money, asking personal questions and so forth. Make sure your beliefs support selling success and align with your organization's values and beliefs around selling and customer service.

Practice and Application

1. Write down the beliefs that support your work and success as a salesperson.

2. What values, beliefs and commitments do you have in common with your organization? *For example, a belief that strong relationships create long-term clients.*

---

2. Be careful about how much time you spend on building a relationship when on a sales call. Always have a desired outcome that *you want* from a sales call and follow *your* sales process. That will help you stay on track for what you need to accomplish.

   A sales process describes the steps taken to sell a prospect from the moment the prospect contacts your company, or you contact them, until services are no longer provided for that client.

Practice and Application

1. Does your organization have a clearly defined sales process? If so, list the steps of that process.

2. If your organization does not have a defined sales process, what process do you go through in selling to a prospect? Define the steps below:
   a.
   b.
   c.
   d.
   e.
   f.
   g.

---

3. Recognize when you are too involved in meeting a prospect or client's needs or helping him or her too much. Set appropriate boundaries between what you can and can not do for the prospect or client.

4. Be very clear as to what the company's offerings are and don't overpromise because you are thinking that you can fix it later. When in doubt as to whether you can meet a particular need, always give yourself an out by saying, "I'm not sure that this is something we can do, so let me check before I say yes or no."

5. Stay objective when working with prospects or clients and remember that a "no" is not a reflection of you as a person; it is just a decision to not buy the services proposed. It's not personal even though it may feel personal.

6. Be very clear about what you want and need especially from the relationships you build. Be honest about what you want out of your investment of time, effort or resources and set expectations upfront so as not to place false or unrealistic expectations on a relationship that leave you feeling taken advantage of, frustrated or even hurt.

7. Let the prospect or client describe what will meet their needs. Ask questions to elicit their desires or needs. This is a serious trap for someone who believes that they know what someone else needs.

8. Stay on track with the appropriate emotions. Knowing that some people buy from the emotional level, be certain that the prospect or client's needs fit the sales situation satisfactorily, not necessarily the emotions connected to the business at hand.

WAKE-UP 30-DAY CHALLENGE

If you really want to see different results, commit to this 30-day challenge and get ready to see transformation before your eyes!

Directions: For the next 30 days, take 15 minutes a day to write down your responses to the questions below. Find a quiet place to write and get yourself a journal to record your thoughts.

Below are two sets of questions. Each day, alternate between the two sets. For example, on day one, respond to Questions 1; on day two respond to Questions 2; on day three respond to Questions 1; on day four respond to Questions 2; and so forth.

Questions 1

1. Where did you and your prospect or client's needs align today?

2. When did you not get what you wanted?

3. Did you ask for what you wanted today?

4. What could have happened if you did?

Questions 2

1. When did you give too much today?

2. When did you give too little?

3. When did you become overemotional and too involved in relationships today?

4. What impact did your reactions and involvement have on you?

Style 3
The Performer

General Characteristics

The Performer is focused on achievement, success, recognition and image. This style thrives in a fast-paced environment where employees earn value and are paid well for what they do, what they achieve and what they accomplish. Winning is paramount, and failure is avoided at all costs. The 3 style projects a high-profile image concerned with who's who, social standings, credentials and status. This style has the ability to shift the image they project to fit the situation: If you are with bankers, you are impeccably dressed; if you are in a biker's bar, you might have on a leather jacket and boots and so forth.

The 3 style is results-oriented. The priority is to be efficient and save time, even if that means cutting corners to get done. The 3 style loves to do several things at once and takes pride in being able to multi-task often attending to the details later. There is an emphasis placed on what was produced versus the finished product, often frustrating others such as the Perfectionists of the world who take pride in the perfect end product. The Performer becomes angry when tasks and goals are interrupted, leaving people and relationships overlooked until the tasks are done. For the 3 style, perhaps in the process of growing up, their "inner child" received the message that they were loved for what was done, not for who they really were. As a result, the Performer as an adult may believe at some level, "I am what I produce."

Sales Environment

The 3 personality in sales is highly valued in today's culture because of the ability to juggle many things at once, meet deadlines, produce results and create the right image for the prospect or client. The gift of this style is the attention to results. Style 3 proves over and over that they can win!

The challenges in selling facing this Style include:

- Focusing on the task and rushing rapport-building with a prospect or client in order to get to the end results. This approach may communicate negative messages when trying to establish and maintain rapport.

- Having difficulty listening to the prospect or client. Feeling very confident in the self and one's abilities, the 3 style has difficulty sitting still and listening or even being present to a prospect or client when needed.

- Overpromising so as not to be perceived as merely helpful, but to get what the 3 seller wants—the sale! The thinking goes like this: Details can be figured out later.

- Creating unhappy internal relationships because you are always trying to get what you promised the client, even when it's outside the boundaries of the company's services.

- Having difficulty saying no to the prospect or client and not being honest upfront with what you can and can not do.

- Overcommitting, making too many promises that keep you racing for time to accomplish what you have promised within an agreed upon timeframe. The latter behaviors usually result in missing or running late for meetings, missing deadlines and, in general, being unpredictable and unreliable. Co-workers may suffer as well, especially if they are viewed as less important than prospects or clients or the sales deal on the table.

- Forgetting important details during the sales process. While the 1 style may spend too much time on details, the 3 style may not spend enough attention to details and walk away from a sales meeting not having the full information needed to move forward.

- Neglecting to self-observe an underlying avoidance of handling emotions during the sales process, has the effect of creating difficulty getting to real problems that the prospect or client may be facing

WAKE-UP Strategies for the 3 Style

1. Be aware of the beliefs you hold regarding being a salesperson, dealing with emotions, asking personal questions and so forth. Make sure your beliefs support selling success and align with your organization's values and beliefs about selling and customer service.

Practice and Application

1. Write down the beliefs that support your work and success as a salesperson.

2. What values, beliefs and commitments do you have in common with your organization? *For example, a belief that strong relationships create long-term clients.*

---

2. Schedule enough time in between meetings to allow for spending enough time at an appointment and not having to rush through a sales call.

A sales process describes the steps taken to sell a prospect from the moment the prospect contacts your company, or you contact them, until services are no longer provided for that client.

Practice and Application

1. Does your organization have a clearly defined sales process? If so, list the steps of that process.

2. If your organization does not have a defined sales process, what process do you go through in selling to a prospect? Define the steps below:
   a.
   b.
   c.
   d.
   e.
   f.
   g.

---

3.   Follow through the sales process without rushing so that you don't miss steps or important details.

4.   Learn that there is a difference between who you are as a person and what you do (your role). Learn how to distinguish between the two.

5.   Make doing paperwork an integral task. Realize that when working with others who support your efforts, they can't read your mind or interpret what you want—you need to be clear with details and put as much as possible in writing so that everyone is on the same page.

6.   Be very clear as to what the company's offerings are and don't overpromise. Avoid having to come back later and take away something you promised.

7.   Make time for people in your schedule. Spend some time nurturing the relationships that count, especially with your co-workers and family members who support your efforts.

8.   Practice self-honesty. The truth will set you free. Note your tendency to embellish, particularly around how you appear to others.

9.   Slow down and learn to relax.

WAKE-UP 30-DAY CHALLENGE

If you really want to see different results, commit to this 30-day challenge and get ready to see transformation before your eyes!

Directions: For the next 30 days, take 15 minutes a day to write down your responses to the questions below. Find a quiet place to write and get yourself a journal to record your thoughts.

Below are two sets of questions. Each day, alternate between the two sets. For example, on day one, respond to Questions 1; on day two respond to Questions 2; on day three respond to Questions 1; on day four respond to Questions 2; and so forth.

Questions 1

1. Where did you win today?

2. Where did you avoid failure?

3. How did you feel about yourself and about your role as a salesperson today? Using a scale of one to five (1-5), with one being horrible and 5 being great, write in your choice and then explain why you rated yourself this way. (Refer to #4 Wake-Up Strategy.)

Self: _____ Why?

Salesperson: _____ Why?

Questions 2

1. How did I avoid uncovering and dealing with my prospect or client's emotions today?

2. What could have happened if you allowed these emotions to surface?

Style 4
The Romantic

General Characteristics

The Romantic is a self-starter whose attention is pulled toward what's missing or wrong; deep, intense relationships; and being viewed as unique. This style tends to be drawn to professions that allow for creativity, individual expression and authentic relationships. The 4 style wants distinctive work that calls for creativity, even genius, an eccentric edge in presentation and a unique approach to business life. Work is valuable when meaningful, authentic and unique. Balancing the checkbook or doing paperwork are considered mundane tasks. These tasks may never make it to the to-do-list because they are not unique and therefore not really valuable through the lens of the Romantic.

The 4 style notices what others have and what they do not have. This style may think that if only they had "it", they would be complete or happy. The Romantic thrives on drama and intense emotions and has the ability to be with people and their emotions whether high or low. Emotions may be experienced as fact and may override one's ability to get work done, complete mundane tasks or achieve goals. When emotions are engaged in a positive sense, the 4 style is productive, highly energized and engaged.

Sales Environment

The Romantic as a salesperson is highly productive when focused on unique, meaningful and creative work. For a Romantic to be successful in sales, he or she must be selling products or services that make a difference and that require them to be creative or aesthetically engaged.

The challenges that this style faces in selling include:

- Becoming bored with following a sales process because it may not allow for artistic or creative expression. Consequently, the relationship involved may take front and center and the details of closing a deal may get lost.
- Making small talk and schmoozing are boring ways to spend time and, therefore, Romantics won't waste their time building social rapport. "Let's get down to the deep emotional stuff—the real issues."
- Focusing too much on the emotions or lack of emotions that are created during the sales process is the downside. This style may create a drama just to rev up the relationship and get some movement toward resolution.
- Depending on how they feel, the Romantic can be immobilized or delay important tasks when not feeling right. "I'm not in the mood" is often heard from disengaged 4s.
- Taking a "no" as a personal affront and feeling personally rejected by others can easily occur.
- Assuming everyone wants the same level of emotional intensity and relationship. Others styles often feel overwhelmed by the 4's need for deep and meaningful connection.

WAKE-UP Strategies for the 4 Style

1. Be aware of the beliefs you hold regarding being a salesperson, discussing money, asking personal questions and so forth. Make sure your beliefs support selling success and align with your organization's values and beliefs about selling and customer service.

Practice and Application

1. Write down the beliefs that support your work and success as a salesperson.

2. What values, beliefs and commitments do you have in common with your organization? *For example, a belief that strong relationships create long-term clients.*

---

2. Balance the amount of time you spend relating or dealing with feelings versus time moving through the sales process and getting to the desired outcomes.

A sales process describes the steps taken to sell a prospect from the moment the prospect contacts your company, or you contact them, until services are no longer provided for that client.

Practice and Application

1. Does your organization have a clearly defined sales process? If so, list the steps of that process.

2. If your organization does not have a defined sales process, what process do you go through in selling to a prospect? Define the steps below:

   a.

   b.

   c.

   d.

   e.

   f.

   g.

---

3. Keep focusing and moving forward when emotions seem overwhelming. Pay attention to when you are giving too much credence to emotions: They may blind you to what's really going on. By staying on task, you'll find an increased ability to sort through the emotions as you are getting things done.

4. Name your emotions rather than be them. Simply naming emotions helps create objectivity and a chance to make a choice as to how much control they will have over you.

5. The next time you are overwhelmed by emotions, ask yourself why you are feeling this way? Is it out of emotional habit? What are you avoiding? Ordinariness? Mundane responsibilities? Getting your work done? What appears to be missing?

6. Stay focused on the desired outcome of a sales call.

7. Follow the sales process so that you don't miss the important, mundane details.

8. Don't take everything so personally. Try to be more objective when dealing with others.

WAKE-UP 30-DAY CHALLENGE

If you really want to see different results, commit to this 30-day challenge and get ready to see transformation before your eyes!

Directions: For the next 30 days, take 15 minutes a day to write down your responses to the questions below. Find a quiet place to write and get yourself a journal to record your thoughts.

Below are two sets of questions. Each day, alternate between the two sets. For example, on day one, respond to Questions 1; on day two respond to Questions 2; on day three respond to Questions 3; on day four respond to Questions 1; on day five respond to Questions 2; and so forth.

Questions 1

1. How did your emotions derail you today?

Questions 2

1. When didn't you feel good enough?

2. What impact did that have on you and your results today?

Questions 3

1. When did you get bored today?

2. What business did you accomplish today?

Style 5
The Observer

General Characteristics

The Observer values autonomy, privacy and self-sufficiency. This style views the world as demanding and invasive and responds by seeking privacy, limiting desires and gathering lots of information. The Observer views knowledge as power and the pursuit of ideas, information and more knowledge is the way to gain power and predictability in an unpredictable and demanding world. Information is held tightly and given out only when necessary. Logic, order and structure are valued in the business world; emotions are inappropriate and to be experienced in private. There is an avoidance or intolerance for issues that might create an emotional response in others. Likewise, this style limits interactions with others, engaging only when absolutely necessary, preferring written communication above talking, closed doors and as few meetings as possible.

The 5 style thrives in an environment where autonomy, independence and self-sufficiency are valued, and decision making is based on facts, logic and reason. The Observer has the ability to be calm in a crisis, remain objective from a detached perspective and think logically for solutions.

Sales Environment

The Observer as a salesperson is knowledgeable about product and services and believes that the prospect or client should have all the facts before making a decision to buy. This style thrives in sales when interactions are limited to a few and the need for influence and selling is minimal. The 5 style has the ability to remain detached from the outcome of the sale and can gather the necessary information needed to determine what the prospect or client wants and needs.

The challenges that this style faces in selling include:

- Has difficulty in creating rapport with a prospect or new player. Dislikes small talk and feels uncomfortable asking personal questions.
- Wants to demonstrate knowledge and expertise, and often gives out too much information and overwhelms the buyer.
- Asks lots of questions to gather information, but shies away from questions that seem too personal especially money, how the decision will be made and the personal reasons for buying.
- Likes the sales call to be orderly and predictable. Follows a sales process if they believe in it.
- Prefers one-on-one interactions to group or team selling.
- Hates to be observed and is uncomfortable selling in the presence of others. Makes it difficult for others to provide feedback necessary to improve selling skills.

WAKE-UP Strategies for the 5 Style

1. Become aware of the beliefs you hold regarding being a sales person, discussing money, asking personal questions and so forth. You could be your own worst enemy when it comes to your beliefs about selling!

2. Have a clearly defined sales process. Because you have the ability to stay detached emotionally, having a sales process is an excellent tool that keeps you on track and focused on the outcome—a sale!

   A sales process describes the steps taken to sell a prospect from the moment the prospect contacts your company, or you contact them, until services are no longer provided for that client.

Practice and Application

1. Write down the beliefs that support your work and success as a salesperson.

2. What values, beliefs and commitments do you have in common with your organization? *For example, a belief that strong relationships create long-term clients.*

Practice and Application

1. Does your organization have a clearly defined sales process? If so, list the steps of that process.

2. If your organization does not have a defined sales process, what process do you go through in selling to a prospect? Define the steps below:
   a.
   b.
   c.
   d.
   e.
   f.
   g.

3. Develop specific strategies for dealing with the initial few minutes of a sales call with a prospect. How will you introduce yourself? What are the first few questions you can ask to build rapport? Preview the situation in your thoughts.

4. View rapport building as information gathering that leads to specific results.

5. Watch your urge to give out too much information or prescribe too early in the sales process.

6. Share your thought process with the prospect or client—not just your recommendations. For example, "Here's what I've observed and here's what I can recommend based on that observation." This style thinks and then quickly reaches conclusions, thereby making it difficult for others to buy into recommendations they have not talked through in order to arrive at a thoughtful conclusion.

7. Avoid making assumptions or judgments about what the prospect or client wants. Have a prepared set of questions that elicits the information from the prospect or client.

8. Pay attention to your body language when selling. Because privacy is so important personally, you may convey your discomfort to people who will be asking what you perceive as personal questions. Be careful not to take on a closed stance or to hesitate around asking questions that make you feel uncomfortable.

WAKE-UP 30-DAY CHALLENGE

If you really want to see different results, commit to this 30-day challenge and get ready to see transformation before your eyes!

Directions: For the next 30 days, take 15 minutes a day to write down your responses to the questions below. Find a quiet place to write and get yourself a journal to record your thoughts.

Below are two sets of questions. Each day, alternate between the two sets. For example, on day one, respond to Questions 1; on day two respond to Questions 2; on day three respond to Questions 1; on day four respond to Questions 2; and so forth.

Questions 1

1. When did you withhold yourself, information or your expertise today?

2. What did you accomplish by withholding?

Questions 2

1. When did you shut down in relating to your prospects or clients today?

2. How did you build rapport with your prospects or clients today?

Style 6
The Loyal Skeptic

General Characteristics

Loyal Skeptics are excellent troubleshooters whose attention is drawn to potential danger, doubting and questioning as a way of developing certainty. They ask lots of questions as a way to uncover hidden agendas and the real intentions or motivation behind someone's behavior and thinking. They often feel that others don't see the potential dangers in a situation, business strategy and so forth, and that it is their job to help others see what could go wrong, the pitfalls, or consequences of a decision. This style thrives in underdog situations and is extremely loyal to friends and dutiful about their responsibilities. They either overvalue or undervalue authority's power—either with or against them. Fear is the core driver of this style and is demonstrated through their questioning style, search for certainty and their attention to worst-case thinking.

The 6 style thrives in an environment that encourages discussion and values input from others before making a decision, and in situations in which leaders are consistent and tell the truth (good or bad). Likewise, the 6 style is comfortable when they are not afraid to put the real issues on the table, and when there are clear lines of authority, precisely defined expectations and rewards for being loyal.

Sales Environment

The Loyal Skeptics are skilled at getting to the real reasons a prospect or client wants to buy. They aren't afraid to ask the tough questions and have an intuitive sense of what the client or prospect needs. They prefer to deal with people they know or to whom they have been referred, versus having to prospect or do cold calling. Skilled at building solid relationships, they create a level of trust in others that is demonstrated by their loyalty and commitment to finding the right solutions for the buyer.

The challenges that this style faces in selling include:

- Their questioning style may appear too direct and drilling, which may inhibit the development of rapport.
- They may not listen fully to what the client or prospect wants and, instead, push what they think the client or prospect needs.
- They may be uncomfortable selling to people in authority and in powerful positions.
- They have a start and stop approach to work and projects that can frustrate others and themselves.
- They get to the real issues so quickly sometimes that they don't realize that they do not have all the information they need.
- Their prospects and clients want to not only solve problems but also to move toward a better vision of their current reality. The 6 style can overlook this aspect if they don't pay attention.
- The Loyal Skeptic can be perceived as having a contrary nature. This perception is not the best frame of mind when rapport-building is at stake.
- The style 6 may use humor at the wrong time.
- They may be avoiding observation of their own personal desires.
- They may avoid a high level of success because success may create fear of becoming overwhelmed or invaded.

WAKE-UP Strategies for the 6 Style

1. Become aware of the beliefs you hold regarding being a salesperson, discussing money, asking personal questions and so forth. Make sure your beliefs support selling success and align with your organization's values and beliefs about sales and customer service. Learn that your skills are highly valuable and that you deserve the success you desire.

Practice and Application

1. Write down the beliefs that support your work and success as a salesperson.

2. What values, beliefs and commitments do you have in common with your organization? *For example, a belief that strong relationships create long-term clients.*

---

2. Recognize that your need to feel safe may get in the way of following your sales process. Too often this style spends too much time on rapport and runs out of time to ask for the sale.

   A sales process describes the steps taken to sell a prospect from the moment the prospect contacts your company, or you contact them, until services are no longer provided for that client.

3. Use softening statements before asking questions. For example: "I need to ask you a tough question, is that okay?"

4. Don't be afraid to point out pitfalls or problems but balance it with the positive things as well. Present worst-case and best case scenarios!

Practice and Application

1. Does your organization have a clearly defined sales process? If so, list the steps of that process.

2. If your organization does not have a defined sales process, what process do you go through in selling to a prospect? Define the steps below:
   a.
   b.
   c.
   d.
   e.
   f.
   g.

---

5. Use the word and rather than but. For example, "I see your idea *and* I wonder if you have also considered this possibility?"

6. Spend more time listening to the buyer's wants and reasons for buying.

7. Have a clearly defined goal for each sales call. If you are doubtful of yourself or your situation, you may lose your focus and have difficulty finding your way through the sales call or the prospect or client will have led the dance.

8. Pay attention when you observe yourself procrastinating or putting off doing tasks. Procrastination for this style occurs when there is doubt about a situation. Make certain that you are in agreement with what is expected of you and have clarity around all the factors involved.

9. Trust your instincts and, at the same time, check them out before acting on them. More often than not you are "right on"; therefore, talk the situation out with someone you trust. In this manner, you will gain greater clarity before taking action.

WAKE-UP 30-DAY CHALLENGE

If you really want to see different results, commit to this 30-day challenge and get ready to see transformation before your eyes!

Directions: For the next 30 days, take 15 minutes a day to write down your responses to the questions below. Find a quiet place to write and get yourself a journal to record your thoughts.

Below are two sets of questions. Each day, alternate between the two sets. For example, on day one, respond to Questions 1; on day two respond to Questions 2; on day three respond to Questions 1; on day four respond to Questions 2; and so forth.

Questions 1

1. What doubts and fears did you have today?

2. How did these doubts and fears impact your results today?

Questions 2

1. What did you do well today?

2. Describe a situation where you felt self-confident today?

3. What could happen if you could be that self-confident more often?

Style 7
The Epicure

General Characteristics

The 7 style thinks big picture; can synthesize a large amount of information and distill it all down to a few sentences; wants to keep their options open; and thrives in a fast-paced, fun-filled work environment where there are few limitations and many rewards for thinking outside the box, being innovative and coming up with solutions. This style sees the possibilities of a situation and often avoids looking at the negative or down side. Full of ideas, the 7 style generates lots of ideas yet prefers not to be the one to implement or follow through with them. They get easily bored and have difficulty staying with or seeing something through to fruition. Their energy is up, positive and they are enjoyable to be around. They like to keep their options open; thus, they have difficulty committing too much of themselves for fear of missing a better option.

The Epicure thrives in a work environment with few rules and regulations, where creativity and innovation are valued and authority is viewed as equal.

Sales Environment

Being in sales *is* fun and games to the 7 personality. This style has the capacity to think big in sales, enjoys dealing with the movers and shakers and persons in high positions of authority. Furthermore, they like to make a sale and move on to the next experience. They are creative in proposing solutions and have the ability to influence the buyer by laying out the possibilities that solutions will bring them.

The challenges facing this style in selling include:

- They are able to impress the prospect or client yet have difficulty listening to what the prospect or client wants or needs. Style 7 salespersons believe their ideas are the best.
- Their pace is very fast and may put off or break rapport with those who prefer a slower pace.
- They may discount or not listen to the concerns or objections the buyer may have.
- They may overwhelm the buyer with too many ideas.
- They may think agreement with their ideas means buyer will buy.
- They spend a great deal of time talking and may not get to the important details necessary to complete the sales process.
- They can be unpredictable and often "just a few minutes late" for appointments; they have a tendency to overbook and overpromise time.
- They tend to get bored if the deal takes too long to close.
- They may come across as arrogant or aloof.
- The 7 style has a hard time staying the course with a business deal, especially when in a team situation.
- They may overlook the details that are important to many buyers.

WAKE-UP Strategies for the 7 Style

1. Become aware of the beliefs you hold regarding being a salesperson, discussing money, asking personal questions and so forth. Make sure your beliefs support selling success and align with your organization's values and beliefs about sales and customer service.

Practice and Application

1. Write down the beliefs that support your work and success as a salesperson.

2. What values, beliefs and commitments do you have in common with your organization? *For example, a belief that strong relationships create long-term clients.*

---

2. Follow the sales process. It is a guide for making certain you don't forget important details and keeping you focused on the process at hand.

   A sales process describes the steps taken to sell a prospect from the moment the prospect contacts your company, or you contact them, until services are no longer provided for that client.

3. Watch the tendency to overpromise. Set realistic expectations.

4. Listen to what the prospect or client wants; ask questions rather than giving ideas.

Practice and Application

1. Does your organization have a clearly defined sales process? If so, list the steps of that process.

2. If your organization does not have a defined sales process, what process do you go through in selling to a prospect? Define the steps below:
   a.
   b.
   c.
   d.
   e.
   f.
   g.

---

5. Think about closure in advance. What needs to happen in this meeting to achieve a closed sale?

6. Remember not every idea has to be voiced. When thinking out loud let others know you are doing just that—thinking out loud. This helps others distinguish between an idea and something that must be acted upon immediately.

7. Listen to objections, concerns and so forth and watch the tendency to discount or negate concerns of others.

8. Learn to really care about the concerns of others.

9. Discover that what you view as negative emotions actually may be valuable to getting the sales deal.

WAKE-UP 30-DAY CHALLENGE

If you really want to see different results, commit to this 30-day challenge and get ready to see transformation before your eyes!

Directions: For the next 30 days, take 15 minutes a day to write down your responses to the questions below. Find a quiet place to write and get yourself a journal to record your thoughts.

Below are two sets of questions. Each day, alternate between the two sets. For example, on day one, respond to Questions 1; on day two respond to Questions 2; on day three respond to Questions 1; on day four respond to Questions 2; and so forth.

Questions 1

1. What negative sales situation did you discount or avoid today?

2. What could have happened had you acknowledged the situation?

Questions 2

1. How did you stay focused today?

2. What results did you get from that focus?

Style 8
The Protector

General Characteristics

This style is concerned with power, who has it and who is using it. Attention for the style 8 goes to whoever is in control, or not being controlled by others, and is concerned about authority being fair and just. The school-yard bully in earlier years, style 8 protects those who are viewed as weaker and in need of protection. Protectors are results-oriented, natural born leaders and very confident of their abilities. They are intolerant of those who hide information, try to coverup or manipulate others. Ironically, they often do this themselves. They like intense work and freedom to get to the truth. Their intensity shows in their overwhelming energy that often is easily expressed as anger and directed at others around them. While very supportive of team members, the Protector style typically makes decisions independently of input from others and, as leaders, they believe that their authority is absolute. However, once they have delegated authority they expect their people to make decisions without a lot of handholding. Their style is typically confrontational, direct and assertive in interactions with others. They have high energy and can be great fun to work with.

The 8 style thrives in a work environment where they are the leader and can control their own destiny. Honest feedback is appreciated by this type, as are situations in which anger is accepted. For the Protector types, the fewer the rules the better they like it. They prefer clearly defined expectations and little supervision with accountability processes already in place.

Sales Environment

The 8 salesperson is results-oriented, confident and in charge during the sales call. People of this type are skilled at assessing who the decision makers are and are comfortable selling to those with power. Their energy is big, sometimes overwhelming; it communicates a self-assured individual who is in charge and knows what they are talking about. This Style works very hard and intensely, often to the point of exhaustion in an effort to achieve desired results.

The challenges that this style faces in selling include:

- Taking charge too soon or inappropriately in selling situations. This stance may overwhelm or intimidate the buyer.
- Becoming frustrated with indecisive buyers.
- Being so focused on the results that they skip or blow off the prospect's or client's real issues or concerns.
- Being so directive (bossy!) that buyers feel they are being told what to do.
- Sometimes saying the wrong thing at the wrong time due to being angry.
- Not being comfortable with a range of emotions that prospects or clients may experience during the sales process.
- Coming across as overly confident, even bordering on being brash.
- Having the tendency to become impatient during a long sales process.
- Pushing too hard to get a decision.

WAKE-UP Strategies for the 8 Style

1. Become aware of the beliefs you hold regarding being a sales person, discussing money, asking personal questions and so forth. Make sure your beliefs support selling success and align with your organization's values and beliefs about sales and customer service.

Practice and Application

1. Write down the beliefs that support your work and success as a salesperson.

2. What values, beliefs and commitments do you have in common with your organization? *For example, a belief that strong relationships create long-term clients.*

---

2. You are great at getting results but, as you seek to get results with prospects or clients, remember that your sales process needs to include time for the prospect or client to reflect and think about what is important to them. Don't rush your sales process; rather, be intentional in allowing moments of silence and pause to allow time for the prospect or client to respond to your questions.

   Do you have a defined sales process? If not, do the Practice and Application exercise to define your sales process.

Practice and Application

1. Does your organization have a clearly defined sales process? If so, list the steps of that process.

2. If your organization does not have a defined sales process, what process do you go through in selling to a prospect? Define the steps below:
   a.
   b.
   c.
   d.
   e.
   f.
   g.

---

3. Learn to manage your energy when in a selling situation. Recognize the body language of the prospect or client in order to evaluate the intensity of your energy level.

4. Listen to what the prospect or client wants; ask questions with the intention of exploring their specific needs and desires, rather than telling them what is needed.

5. Request permission to ask questions and be patient when the other individual is speaking. Be aware of the tendency to

"bulldoze" your way to the closure because this behavior will probably intimidate or turn others off.

6. Engage prospects or clients in coming up with the solution rather than telling them what to do.

7. Pay attention to your gut and do your homework so that you are prepared for sales calls. Usually, you are very comfortable winging it, but often what is called for is a mixture of gut (responding in the moment) and information and details that demonstrate your understanding of the prospect or client's situation.

8. When errors occur, either after a sale or during the servicing of the client, avoid blaming others in front of the client. The client isn't concerned with who is at fault; they just want you to fix the problem.

9. Build into your approach some downtime to recharge your energy. Remember that going full speed to the point of dropping is not in your or other's best interest.

WAKE-UP 30-DAY CHALLENGE

If you really want to see different results, commit to this 30-day challenge and get ready to see transformation before your eyes!

Directions: For the next 30 days, take 15 minutes a day to write down your responses to the questions below. Find a quiet place to write and get yourself a journal to record your thoughts.

Below are two sets of questions. Each day, alternate between the two sets. For example, on day one, respond to Questions 1; on day two respond to Questions 2; on day three respond to Questions 1; on day four respond to Questions 2; and so forth.

Questions 1

1. Where did you lose your patience with prospects, clients or other employees today?

2. How did this reaction impact your results today?

3. How did this reaction impact your relationships with these people today?

Questions 2

1. When was your energy too much today?

2. What might have happened if you had softened your energy?

Style 9
The Mediator

General Characteristics

The Mediator is concerned with keeping the peace, avoiding conflict and making sure everyone gets along. Persons of this style are able to understand other points of view, so much so that they tend to adopt another's point of view and avoid having one of their own. They thrive in a work environment that creates structure, guidelines for how conflict is handled and appreciation for input from everyone. They have difficulty prioritizing their workload and see all priorities as equal. Consequently, they may procrastinate or avoid doing tasks if they do not agree with or like them. They do not feel as important as others, nor do they know the next step to take. They don't like being forced to make decisions; rather, they need time to get opinions and gather information. Once a decision is made, there is little movement or change from their position. They are natural team members who are energized by the team's purpose and energy. Left on their own, they have difficulty identifying their agenda, getting tasks done for themselves and staying in action.

Sales Environment

The Mediator is excellent at creating rapport and making people feel comfortable. They are good listeners and are comfortable selling to people they know. They tend to operate intuitively in selling situations, responding to the signals and cues sent by the buyer. They enjoy espousing their personal values and beliefs, and have the ability to bond and sell easily to like-minded people.

The challenges that this style faces in selling include:

- They spend too much time building rapport.

- They get caught up in the buyer's agenda and lose sight of their own agenda for the sales call.
- They have difficulty asking tough or personal questions for fear of creating conflict or upsetting the prospect or client.
- They lack enough energy to stay motivated for selling.
- When they lose their personal agenda, they can get off track, avoiding responsibility and forgetting the important things to complete.
- When conflict arises, they tend to avoid interaction hoping the conflict will go away, or they may try to overcome conflict in a passive-aggressive manner.
- They have difficulty making decisions or presenting solutions that might create conflict, disapproval or rejection by the buyer.
- They get caught up in the moment and lose track of time and the agenda.
- They run out of time to accomplish the desired outcome.

WAKE-UP Strategies for the 9 Style

1. Become aware of the beliefs you hold regarding being a salesperson, discussing money, asking personal questions and so forth. Make sure your beliefs support selling success and align with your organization's values and beliefs about sales and customer service.

2. Stay in control during the sales call by following your sales process.

    A sales process describes the steps taken to sell a prospect from the moment the prospect contacts your company, or you contact them, until services are no longer provided for that client.

Practice and Application

1. Write down the beliefs that support your work and success as a salesperson.

2. What values, beliefs and commitments do you have in common with your organization? *For example, a belief that strong relationships create long-term clients.*

Practice and Application

1. Does your organization have a clearly defined sales process? If so, list the steps of that process.

2. If your organization does **not have a** defined **sales** process, what process do you go through in selling to a prospect? Define the steps below:
   a.
   b.
   c.
   d.
   e.
   f.
   g.

3. Learn to match the energy of your prospect or client. You may need to rev up your own energy in these situations.

4. Watch for zoning or spacing out. Catch yourself and ask, "What am I avoiding?"

5. Be clear about what you agree with and state your disagreement to ensure that you are understood so that no false assumptions or conclusions are drawn by the buyer.

6. Look at how you define conflict. Redefine conflict so that it means a healthy discussion for the purpose of discovering the truth, the real issues needing to be addressed.

7. Develop specific action steps, then break them down and schedule them for completion. Get a deadline from others in order to create a sense of urgency for yourself. If you respond well to deadlines, then intentionally place deadlines on yourself so that you will have to deliver what you promise.

8. Pay attention to your tendency to dig in your heels when you disagree with someone or something you have to do. In this instance, it's time to speak up rather than passively resist!

WAKE-UP 30-DAY CHALLENGE

If you really want to see different results, commit to this 30-day challenge and get ready to see transformation before your eyes!

Directions: For the next 30 days, take 15 minutes a day to write down your responses to the questions below. Find a quiet place to write and get yourself a journal to record your thoughts.

Below are two sets of questions. Each day, alternate between the two sets. For example, on day one, respond to Questions 1; on day two respond to Questions 2; on day three respond to Questions 1; on day four respond to Questions 2; and so forth.

Questions 1

1. When were you stubborn or passive-aggressive today? (Passive-aggressive behavior looks like you are in agreement with someone or you commit to doing something for another when really you don't agree or have no intention of following through with your commitment but you don't say anything to the other person—you either forget or just don't do it.)

2. When did you avoid conflict today? Why?

3. When did you not speak your mind or position today? Why?

Questions 2

1. What was your agenda today?

2. What supported you staying on your agenda today?

Chapter Six

Now That I Know My Style, What Do I Do?

Now that you know your style, self-observation, practice and further exploration begins. Below are some general suggestions for what to do next.

1. If you are having difficulty in discovering your style, request a typing session by calling Mary Anne Wampler at (301) 419-2835. During this 1-1/2 hour session, you'll be led through a process that will help you discover your style.

2. Once you know your style, read some additional resources to confirm and learn more about that style:
    *   *The Enneagram Advantage: Putting the Nine Personality Types to Work in the Office,* by Helen Palmer.
    *   *9 Ways of Working: How to Use the Enneagram to Discover Your Natural Strengths and Work More Effectively,* by Michael J. Goldberg.

- *The Enneagram: Understanding Yourself and Others in Your Life,* by Helen Palmer.
- *The Enneagram in Love and Work: Understanding Your Intimate and Business Relationships,* by Helen Palmer.
- *The Essential Enneagram,* by David Daniels and Virginia Price.

3. In Section 2 of *The Essential Enneagram,* read Part 1 beginning on page 73 and then turn to your specific style in Part 2, which offers practices that help you become more aware of how your personality functions, actions to take to transform your habit of mind, and ways to stay aware and observant of the shifts you are making.

4. Observe yourself and record your observations. Catch yourself in the habit of mind and then reflect on what triggered this reaction. Change begins with self-observation!

5. When you are stressed, feeling defensive, reactive, too intense, no emotions and so forth, step back a few moments to take a look at what's going on, what your reaction is to the situation and what options or choices you have. Then, move back into action.

6. Partner with someone who is also studying the Enneagram and chat regularly about what you are observing with yourself. Hold a lunchtime discussion with individuals of the same style.

7. Look for a local Enneagram community in your area. Many areas are running workshops and evening programs that offer further education and training on the Enneagram.

8. Be open and ask for feedback on how you are affecting others. Reflect on the feedback you get and be inquisitive, rather than judgmental, about why you operate this way.

9. When interacting with others, make no assumptions. Check out other's perceptions, understand what is really being said, and work together to understand each other's point of view.

10. Find 10 minutes every day to quiet yourself, reflect on your observations, reinforce new beliefs and habits and develop strategies that support your professional and personal success.

Sales-Specific Suggestions

1. Debrief after each sales call to determine how you did. Write down observations you had, lessons learned and next actions to take.

2. Ask your sales manager or a mentor to go out on a few sales calls with you so that they can give you feedback not only on sales skills but how you presented yourself, what you did well, what you missed and how you impacted the prospect or client. While difficult to do, this is one of the most effective ways to learn!

3. Plan before going into a sales call and select one challenge that you are going to work on during the call. For instance, if you have difficulty asking for a deposit, commit to not leaving until you ask for it.

4. Be committed to changing old habits into supportive new habits. This means it might get hard to stay committed and

continue the practices, but don't give up! Studies show that it takes at least 21 days to overcome a habit—that is, if you work on it every day.

5. Celebrate when you've been successful or achieved a goal. Celebration reinforces the value of achieving the goal. If you simply move on to just another task or goal, your work might become tedious and uninteresting. Take the time to evaluate the tasks that you have accomplished well. Pat yourself on the back!

Lastly, and above all else, have fun selling!

About Transform, Inc.

Transform, Inc. is committed to developing the job of selling into a profession where salespeople are proud of their profession and view self-development as essential to selling and personal success.

Photography: Inés Younkins

Theresa Gale draws on over 15 years as an organizational consultant, trainer and business owner. Having to sell to build a successful organization, she networks her way to success and is adept at building long-term relationships. Her real talent is in helping organizations build the internal systems necessary to support exceptional client experiences and the training programs that develop client-centered employees. Prior to starting Transform, Inc., Theresa worked as a business consultant and prior to that was the director of operations and administration for a family-owned service operation with revenues of over $22 million, 225 employees and six regional offices on the East Coast.

Photography: Inès Younkins

Mary Anne Wampler has more than 25 years of professional sales experience and for the last decade has dedicated her career to sales training. Mary Anne brings a down-to-earth, real world approach to achieving sales success and draws upon her diverse professional experiences, which include her past role as manager of temporary labor service and as the advertising director of a large newspaper chain. Equipped with a broad range of expertise and skills, Mary Anne empowers sales professionals by helping them to understand the personal stumbling blocks that diminish their success and challenging organizations to offer a more nurturing environment in which their employees can grow.

Transform, Inc. is available to work with companies and individuals who are interested in doing whatever it takes to lead their companies and their sales results to the next level.

If you or someone you know is ready to take the next step, contact us at (301) 419-2835.

What are you waiting for?

Key Learnings To Remember

Key Learnings To Remember

Key Learnings To Remember

ISBN 141203583-X